THIS IS
A BOOK FOR
PEOPLE
WHO LOVE

DOGS

THIS IS
A BOOK FOR
PEOPLE
WHO LOVE

DOGS

MEG FREITAG

ILLUSTRATED BY LUCY ROSE

RUNNING PRESS
PHILADELPHIA

Running Press
Hachette Book Group
1290 Avenue of the Americas, New York, NY 10104
www.runningpress.com
@Running_Press

Printed in China

First Edition: August 2023

Published by Running Press, an imprint of Perseus Books, LLC, a subsidiary of Hachette Book Group, Inc. The Running Press name and logo are trademarks of the Hachette Book Group.

The Hachette Speakers Bureau provides a wide range of authors for speaking events. To find out more, go to www.hachettespeakersbureau.com or email HachetteSpeakers@hbgusa.com.

Running Press books may be purchased in bulk for business, educational, or promotional use. For more information, please contact your local bookseller or the Hachette Book Group Special Markets Department at Special.Markets@hbgusa.com.

The publisher is not responsible for websites (or their content) that are not owned by the publisher.

Print book cover and interior design by Jenna McBride.

Library of Congress Control Number: 2022950842

ISBNs: 978-0-7624-8313-6 (hardcover), 978-0-7624-8316-7 (ebook)

APS

10 9 8 7 6 5 4 3 2 1

For Ramona and Winnie,
my joyfulness increasers.

CONTENTS

WHY WE LOVE DOGS

I f you're reading this book, odds are you like dogs. Love them, even. Maybe you have one or two or five of your own. You might be a small dog person. Or a big dog person. Or a rescue dog person. Perhaps you grew up with a certain breed, and you're carrying the Yorkie (or Saint Bernard or black Lab or dachshund) torch. Or not. I come from a long line of shih tzu people, and yet I share my home with two beautiful, barky, medium-size mutts. Earth angels, I call them. My little blessings. For people like us—dog people—our love  for our pups certainly can border on devotional. Even evangelistic. I suspect I'm not the only dog owner who's cornered someone at a dinner party to talk about her dogs. *Have you heard? Dogs exist.*

In truth, the decision to welcome a dog into one's life is an intricate cost-benefit calculation that each person must make for themselves. The costs certainly aren't negligible. Dogs are messy, and they bark. They can be destructive. You may never travel on a whim again, or eat a meal in peace. And it's worth acknowledging that dog ownership requires a certain degree of situational privilege. They're time-consuming and expensive— sometimes frighteningly so. And yet, for so many of us, the benefits of having a dog around overwhelmingly outweigh the expenses, the limitations, the inconveniences, and, ultimately, the inevitable and considerable heartbreak these brief-ish unions impose on us.

Of course, some dogs benefit us in practical ways— they guard homes, they help with hunting and ranching or farming, or, in the case of service dogs, they help us navigate the world more confidently and safely. And some dogs may represent our livelihood or a passion 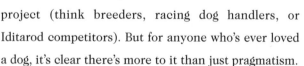 project (think breeders, racing dog handlers, or Iditarod competitors). But for anyone who's ever loved a dog, it's clear there's more to it than just pragmatism.

Dogs appeal to our minds, for one. Their reliance on us can bring structure and purpose to our days. In this way and others, they support our mental health.

Studies have shown that close contact with dogs (petting, playing with them, or even making eye contact) triggers a spike in the feel-good hormone oxytocin. And it's a wonder to simply behold them—their curious behaviors and their odd and singular personalities, the ways in which they're similar to us and yet mesmerizingly different. Dogs entertain us, they keep us busy both physically and mentally, and they draw us out of our shells and encourage us to engage with the world in ways we might not be inclined to otherwise.

Then there's the matter of our hearts. People often talk about the feeling of unconditional love they get from their dogs—an exquisitely uncomplicated love, free from the looming threat of judgment that tinges many of even our dearest human relationships. And *this*, I would argue, is perhaps the most precious benefit of all. Dogs show us that we're fundamentally lovable, despite everything we believe about ourselves to the contrary. Dogs don't care that we picked a fight with someone at work for no reason, or how much reality television we've been watching lately. They don't care about our morning breath, our languishing to-do lists, or the disparaging thing our aunt said about us over the holidays that we fear in our heart of hearts might be true. They love us for who we are and, in doing so, can teach us to see ourselves as worthy of such love. It's something that many seek to find via psychotherapy, psychic hotlines, or ayahuasca retreats in the rain forests of Peru—and yet the evidence is right here with us, in our living room, paws twitching as she naps on the floor in a perfect square of sunlight.

The connection we humans feel to this whole other species is almost mystical in its ubiquity and long history. Since before the advent of literature, mathematics, or agriculture, dogs have been at our side. And not only that, but they have been integral to our progress through the ages. Many scientists believe our species might not have made it this far without them, and vice versa.

So, though this is a book about dogs, it's also a book about us. With dogs, we took something that existed and shined it up until we could see ourselves in it. In myth and literature, this is the stuff of cautionary tales. Narcissus wasted away staring at his reflection in a pool of water, so in love he was with what he saw. But with dogs, we got something right. Perhaps because we had help. Dogs were there, after all—our unhesitating helpers, our comrades, our most forgiving mirrors.

In her 2013 book *Dog Songs*, poet Mary Oliver meditates on just how deep this interspecies love story runs: "Because of the dog's joyfulness, our own is increased. It is no small gift. It is not the least reason why we should honor as well as love the dog of our own life, and the dog down the street, and all the dogs not yet born. What would the world be like without music or rivers or the green and tender grass? What would this world be like without dogs?"

THE DOMESTICATED DOG: AN ORIGIN STORY

When I watch a video of my favorite elderly Instagram pug, Evy, in her pink fleece bunny onesie, trying her best to bite her plush carrot hard enough to make it squeak, it feels irreconcilable that we categorically place her alongside highly trained, drug-sniffing German shepherds or Siberian huskies who can pull heavy sleds for hundreds of miles through the arctic tundra.

And it feels more irreconcilable still to imagine that all these dogs—and in fact every dog on the face of the planet—hail from a single common ancestor, who also happens to be one of humankind's fiercest, most enduring rivals: *Canis lupus*. Wolves. But the DNA evidence is unimpeachable. Dogs as we know them—*Canis lupus familiaris*—are domesticated wolves.

This evidence naturally begs the question of *how*. How did *wolves* evolve into our constant companions, the stars of our Instagram feeds, our very own best boys and girls? Unsatisfyingly, no one can say for sure exactly how (or why or where or when) the process of canine domestication started. There are, however, some theories.

❧ ❧ ❧ ANCIENT HISTORY ❧ ❧ ❧

Wolves were, by a long shot, our first foray into domestication, though the transformation of *Canis lupus* into *Canis familiaris* is a process that took *at least* a thousand generations.

It's likely that our two species encountered each other somewhere in the neighborhood of 45,000 years ago when anatomically modern humans first made their way from Africa to Eurasia, where wolves were already long established as champions of the food chain. Apex predators. These wolves—a yet-unidentified, now-extinct species, believed to be the predecessor to both domesticated dogs *and* modern wolves—likely posed an immediate threat to our ancestors for two reasons: though today's wolves don't typically prey on humans, these prehistoric wolves may have; also, as we were still hunter-gatherers, they would have been our closest resource rivals. And as humans grew in numbers and became more adept at navigating the new terrain, we would have become a threat to them, as well.

Like any good rivalry, however, our antagonism held within itself a kind of shadowy peer status. For how different our two species are in form and function, there are some surprising synchronicities. Our comparable intelligence, for one, and the notable overlap in our diets. We're both widely adaptable to various climates, and both our species exist within complex social groups, involving hierarchy and the assigning of roles, which means—quite significantly—that both wolves and humans are hardwired to work cooperatively. We needed similar things and were similarly positioned to get them. So, what made us a threat to each other is also likely what led us, eventually, to join forces. One might argue that our partnership was inevitable, even destined—like Orion and Sirius, it was written in the stars.

We don't know precisely when this commingling began, and cynologists (the term for those who study domesticated dogs) are divided on which of our two species broke the ice. Did adventurous wolves with docile genes seek us out for our carcass-strewn garbage heaps? And perhaps in doing so, these scavenging wolves found a new way to live well, and met similarly docile, human-curious wolves with whom to breed? Or did we keep wolves in captivity so that we could eat them, wear their pelts, and use them, even, in ritual sacrifice? It's not uncommon for ancient wolf bones to show markings from stone tools. In this proposed scenario, perhaps we killed quickly those who acted aggressively toward us but allowed the less aggressive wolves to live long enough to breed, maybe pardoning those who showed an aptitude for helping us hunt or guard our camps.

Or have we just always had a soft spot for puppies and, at some point, began adopting (or abducting) the fluffy, clumsy, briefly benign pups of our enemies? For dog lovers, the appeal of having playful puppies around requires no imaginative gymnastics. Especially in the primitive, amenity-scant camps of our early nomadic ancestors, the pups would have really had something to offer: Not only would they have cheered and amused us, they'd also have kept us warm. Our first portable space heaters! And perhaps some of these pups grew up to be helpful, tractable adults who were permitted to stick around, eventually spawning families of their own.

As the adage goes, given enough time, everything that *can* happen *will* happen, and there are researchers who believe these various origin hypotheses are in no way mutually exclusive. Perhaps they *all* happened at different points in time, or in different places. It's been argued that the domestication of wolves wasn't a one-time event and occurred spontaneously in separate regions. In truth, it's likely these theories will remain eternally just that—there's no way to know exactly how it all began, short of the invention of a time machine.

But whatever the reason, it was impactful enough to *slowly* begin altering the DNA of those wolves we had consistent contact with, thus kicking off a new hybrid species—a continuously evolving canid that wasn't quite wolf but wasn't yet dog—which evidence shows we coexisted with peaceably for thousands of years.

🐾 🐾 🐾 THE FIRST DOG 🐾 🐾 🐾

We also can't say when the first "true" dog appeared. Despite the physical changes wolves certainly underwent during their long prologue, DNA reigns as the sole determiner of whether a dog-like creature can in fact be classified as *Canis familiaris*. And, because DNA degrades the longer it's around, older archaeological samples don't have the same genetic verification potential as newer ones.

"Newer" is, of course, relative. Indisputably, we know that dogs existed 14,000 years ago. The remains of two genetically verifiable dogs—one just seven months old when it died from canine distemper—were uncovered alongside two adult humans at a Paleolithic-era gravesite, in what is now western Germany. But there's a good chance that dogs have been with us even longer. Much older remains that check some of the right boxes have been found in Siberia, Belgium, and the Middle East, but the DNA isn't complete enough to be conclusive, either way.

The question of the first dog is one that researchers are hopeful they'll someday be able to answer. DNA testing is advancing all the time, and the data we need to unlock the secret of the "first" dog are presumably out there somewhere, waiting to be unearthed. We only have to keep digging—literally.

DNA aside, there's plenty of archaeological evidence that points to our evolving bonds. In France's Chauvet Cave—rendered famous by the 1994 discovery of its Upper Paleolithic cave paintings—archaeologists made a compelling adjacent discovery: fossilized footprints of a human child and a canine walking side by side. Though we'll never know if the four-legged creature was genetically wolf or dog, we can deduce that the child trusted him. There was a closeness between them. What's more, soot on the wall from the child's torch provided a time stamp; this scene took

place 26,000 years ago. Twelve thousand years before our "first" puppy succumbed to his distemper.

🐾🐾🐾 REINVENTING THE DOG 🐾🐾🐾

Compared to humans, many dogs are better runners, swimmers, and trackers. They are stronger, scrappier, and less preoccupied with their own mortality. We've long used their talents for our betterment, augmenting our own capabilities with theirs. In a way, dogs were one of our earliest forms of technology.

As such, for most of our shared history, we bred dogs with job descriptions in mind: they were hunters, foragers, sentinels, soldiers, and sherpas; they pulled sleds and carts, kept homes and ships and churches vermin free, and protected and corralled livestock. This isn't to say we didn't also love them, but they earned their keep.

During the Victorian era, this all changed. Dogfighting was outlawed in the British Isles in 1835, and from the ashes of a terrible spectacle, a new popular form of canine entertainment was born: the dog show. The first show took place in 1859 in Newcastle upon Tyne, and the phenomenon quickly spread throughout England and the British colonies, across Europe, and on to the Americas.

As dog show fever mounted, an increasing number of people grew restless in their spectatorship. There was money to be made and prestige to be had. But there was a twist, and one that would change dogdom forever: Victorians were drunk en masse on the then-groundbreaking evolutionary studies of Charles Darwin. Ambitious hobbyists and entrepreneurs were moved to put Darwin's theories of controlled evolution (in essence, selective breeding) to work on our oldest interspecies friends, with the goal of creating the most show-worthy dogs ever. And, thus, a canine breeding craze began.

While many breeders were content to tinker with existing breeds, others took a more innovative tack and set out to design all-new dogs through interbreeding.

Many of these novelty mixes—known then as *manu-factures*—became prototypes for today's most beloved breeds. In fact, the majority of the breeds we recognize today were manufactures born out of this grand-scale Victorian experiment.

In response to the breeding mania, this period also heralded the formation of kennel clubs—many of which still exist today—whose purpose it was to oversee and maintain breeding standards, officiate new breeds, keep breeding records, and sanction dog shows.

Though humans had been selectively breeding dogs to be better scenters, sighters, runners, retrievers, and killers long before the nineteenth century, the Victorian era was unique for the sheer number of people who took an interest in the project, and for how the focus of breeding shifted throughout the western world. For the first time, dogs weren't bred primarily to be laborers. Now they could also be *pets*.

MEET THE
CANIDAE FAMILY

Domesticated dogs are members of the Canidae family, a distinction shared with thirty-something other living canid (or canine) species. This group of predatory quadrupedal mammals includes wolves, foxes, jackals, coyotes, and dingoes, among some lesser-known others (the rare and evasive South American bush dog and the petite, arboreal raccoon dog, native to East Asia, are a couple examples). The Canidae family is about 40 million years old.

Wild canids can be found on all continents except Antarctica, and, like us, they've adapted to live in forests, tundras, savannahs, deserts, and neighborhoods. In the wild, they range in size from a mere nine inches in length (the fennec fox) to more than seven feet (the gray wolf). Out of the wild, domesticated dogs claim both slots—a teacup Chihuahua is smaller than a fennec fox, and mastiff-type dogs are on average larger than wolves.

Like the unknown prehistoric wolf that spawned both *Canis lupus* and *Canis familiaris*, many canine species that once flourished are now extinct. Through-out the epochs, plenty of canine species disappeared on their own due to natural selection or major climate shifts (e.g., the Ice Age), though humans are largely to blame for more recent extinctions. Because the canine prey drive has repeatedly threatened humans' lives and livelihoods, species have been intentionally culled via hunting, trapping, and poisoning. Rabies scares, too, have been a cause for mass exterminations—a fate that befell the Japanese Honshu wolf—and others, like Alaska's Kenai Peninsula wolf, were poached to obliv-ion for their pelts. Indirectly, habitat loss due to things like suburban sprawl and deforestation has also been an eradicating factor.

Even for many still-existing species, their grip on existence is tenuous—about a third of canine species are considered vulnerable or endangered. Several species—the red wolf and African hunting dog among them—are alive today only by the grace of just-in-time govern-ment protections and/or targeted repopulation efforts. The domesticated dog, on the other hand, is absolutely thriving—to the extent that one might wonder if their ancestors were putting in a prophetic bid for survival when they forged their human unions long ago.

Domesticated dogs share 99.8 percent of their DNA with wolves—their closest living relative—and the two can even mate and produce viable (fertile) hybrid offspring. They're so genetically similar that the domesticated dog isn't considered a distinct species in most classification systems but rather a *sub*species of wolf: *Canis* lupus *familiaris*.

But in many important ways dogs and wolves couldn't be more different. After all, dogs (or the wolf-dogs that would become them) have spent the better part of 40,000 years in proximity to us—cooperating with us, communicating with us, learning our rhythms, and adapting to the domestic sphere. Something of a hybrid species themselves, dogs straddle two worlds—two paws in the wilderness, two paws on the sofa as they lick the leftover peanut butter from our spoon.

DOMESTICATED DOGS VS. WILD CANIDS: SOME DIFFERENCES

Here are a few concrete examples of how domesticated dogs diverge from other canids. In no way meant to be comprehensive, you can think of this section like a flashlight beam grazing a grainy path through a vast and wondrous cynological landscape.

───────── Eternal Puppyhood ─────────

Early on in their evolutionary journey from wolf to dog, wolf-dogs would have begun to retain more and more puppylike—and human-friendly—behavioral traits into adulthood. In other words, they would have progressively become more docile, playful, and curious.

As a by-product of this arrested behavioral development, wolf-dogs would have experienced physical changes, as well. Their adult bodies, too, would have become more puppylike, and this phenomenon accounts for some of the baseline morphological differences between wolves and domesticated dogs: dogs' flopped-over ears and their upturned, wagging tails; their shorter snouts and larger eyes; their bigger head size compared with their bodies. Adult wolves also seldom bark—they're more prone to howling—whereas wolf pups, like dogs, communicate mainly by barking.

Though we don't have records, we know this because *all* domesticated animals experience this juvenilization. An evolutionary phenomenon known as *neoteny*, it's one of the first big stops on the way to tameness.

——— Home Is Where the Humans Are ———

Even feral dogs (which, combined with strays and street dogs, account for a whopping three quarters or more of the dog population worldwide) are inclined to live among humans. Rather than making their homes in forests and grasslands as wild canids do, dogs overwhelmingly tend to inhabit more densely human-populated areas. It's not only that dogs are innately less fearful of people— though this is usually true—but evolution has made it so that dogs no longer possess the survival instincts of other wild canines. They're simply not equipped to fend for themselves in the wilderness.

This doesn't mean dogs are less smart, though. Researchers believe that over the course of their evolution, dogs gradually traded the wolf's inborn problem-solving intelligence for a kind of social and emotional intelligence that benefited them more in the human context. They learned instead how to help and support humans, who in turn sheltered and fed them. This symbiotic dependence on humans is now part of their genetic makeup—even a dog who's never seen the inside of a house is still hardwired to look to humans to fill in the gaps of his unmet needs.

Table-scrap-ivores

Though all canines—dogs included—have the telltale flesh-tearing teeth and bone-dissolving digestive enzymes of carnivores, they're not considered obligate carnivores, meaning their bodies can derive protein and other crucial nutrients from nonmeat food sources. Cats *need* meat to survive; canids do not. As such, canids are often called scavenger carnivores, or "opportunivores." Wild canines frequently supplement their diets with plants, insects, and even the droppings of herbivores when the herbivores themselves are scarce.

Thanks to millennia of sharing food with humans, the diet of domesticated dogs is even more varied. In particular, dogs stand out from other canids in their ability to digest starches—a development that likely occurred on the heels of the Agricultural Revolution, some 10,000 years ago, when humans first widely began growing and storing grain. Today, most commercial dog foods have a high starch content in addition to the requisite animal fats and proteins, and carbohydrates are considered an essential part of a balanced dog diet (though the optimal amount of daily starch varies from breed to breed).

Even in captivity, wolves will typically decline to eat in the presence of humans. It's not news to most of us that dogs, on the other hand, tend to have less discernment when it comes to who witnesses their mealtimes.

DOMESTIC PARTNERS: WHAT DO HUMANS AND DOGS SHARE?

Genetically, we're nothing like dogs. And yet how much time we've spent together has had a transformational influence on both our species. The ways we've evolved to more effectively communicate with and comprehend the other has shaped the development of our brains, and our shared lifestyles and environments have aligned aspects of our biology (as in the example of dogs' digestive systems adapting to a starch-rich diet).

Though we run the risk of misunderstanding dogs if we read ourselves too acutely in them—attributing human intentions, motivations, yearnings, and betrayals to them, for instance—some level of anthropomorphism is inherent in empathy. And we must have empathy. We must risk hubris to let ourselves imagine—however imperfectly—what our dogs are experiencing and feeling so that we can care for them compassionately. The greater danger, I'd say, is in letting ourselves see dogs as fundamentally unfathomable. Much cruelty and abuse has been heaped on dogs (and all nonhuman animals) throughout the ages by those who've reasoned that distress, grief, and pain are uniquely human registers of feeling.

🐾 🐾 🐾 MORE THAN WORDS 🐾 🐾 🐾

Dogs have a surprisingly sophisticated grasp on human language. Though they're unable to interpret much of our *content* (aside from the imperatives we've taught them, and other oft-repeated words and phrases they've picked up), they register tone expertly and can derive much meaning from this alone. But there's more to it than tone. For example, studies have shown that if we experimentally say "bad dog" to a dog in a sweet, cooing voice, dogs will often exhibit signs of confusion. As if they understand, on some level, that the content and container are misaligned. Dogs also know when we're using a foreign language or speaking gibberish.

Humans have an intrinsic understanding of dogs' various vocalizations, too. Even those who aren't intimately familiar with dogs can readily distinguish aggression, fear, pain, and play from their tonal qualities.

Dogs are also masters of interpreting visual cues like body language. Aside from scent, this is the primary way they communicate with each other, and it's also how they get their best read on us. From our posture, gait, and facial expressions, they can determine the general state of our internal affairs. Even puppies have this level of "intuition," suggesting it's not a learned aptitude but something innate.

Dogs and elephants are the only species that know without being taught what humans mean when we point—*look, that over there!*—and will follow an extended finger with their gaze. Some nonhuman primates can develop this skill, but they need to first learn it.

And dogs have evolved to communicate with *us* through visual signaling, though a lot of it hits us at the sub-perceptual level. Dogs' expressive faces are no accident. In particular, the way they widen their eyes— something wolves can't do—was conceived of by evolution to evoke human sympathy, as it lends them an innocent, even helpless, appearance. After all, aren't we far more likely to dote on a pitiful creature than on one we fear might have the strength of character required to turn on us one day?

♣ ♣ IN SICKNESS AND IN HEALTH ♣ ♣

Presumably due to environmental and lifestyle factors we share—not enough exercise? preservatives? asbestos? smog?—dogs develop many of the same diseases that plague modern humans. Cancer and heart disease are the two leading causes of death in both humans and domesticated dogs, for instance, and dogs also experience tumors, arthritis, epilepsy, diabetes, kidney disease, autoimmune disorders, and thyroid issues, to name just a few. After diagnosis, dogs even tend to have similar prognoses and respond to the same treatments and medications. There's evidence that dogs are afflicted by human mental illnesses, as well, like anxiety, depression, PTSD, and obsessive-compulsive disorder.

❀ ❀ ❀ A MYSTERIOUS SENSORIUM ❀ ❀ ❀

As mammals, humans and dogs have the same five senses—sight, smell, taste, hearing, and touch—though, a common paradox, it's in the context of this sameness that our differences become amplified. Here we'll take a brief look at how dogs experience each of their senses compared to us.

Sight

In human ophthalmology terms, dogs would be considered nearsighted. While human vision aims for 20/20, the average dog is closer to 20/75, meaning they need to be twenty feet from an object to see it as well as we do from seventy-five feet. Like so many things, this depends on breed. Labradors, who are often used as guide dogs for the blind, have vision approaching 20/20.

Though visual resolution might be lacking in many, dogs' eyes are keenly sensitive to motion. This is especially so in sighthounds, who were bred to spot and run down distant prey. Dogs also see better in the dark than we do, as they have more retinal rods, larger pupils, and something called *tapetum lucidum*—a reflective membrane that sits behind the retina and increases the amount of light the photoreceptors are able to pick up. This membrane is also why dogs' eyes glow spookily in the dark.

Because of their limited light cones (two), dogs live in a yellow and blue world. Everything else is shades of gray. If you've noticed that dogs show preference for blue and yellow toys, this is why—they don't vanish grayly into the gray grass as the red and orange toys do. Humans see a wider color spectrum—one that includes red and orange—thanks to an additional cone. (But beware of getting too puffed up about your three cones—the mantis shrimp, by contrast, has *sixteen*.)

Smell

Dogs are to the smelling world what mantis shrimp are to the color-vision world. How can we begin to imagine colors we've never seen? A dog's sense of smell is similarly inconceivable to us from where we sit, with our woeful five million scent receptors. The average dog, by comparison, has 300 million; not only that, but the olfactory processing area of their brain is forty times larger than

ours. And scenthounds that were
bred to track other animals by
scent have considerably more
olfactory real estate—likely
many times that of the "average" dog.

As a supplement to body language, dogs communicate with each other richly through scent. In human
terms, you can think of it like verbal language versus
written language. Dogs use visual cues—posture, tail
carriage, ear and eye position, facial expressions, etc.—
to transmit information when they're face to face, and
scent is how they leave missives for each other. They
dispatch these missives—which include details about
their age, sex, mood, and health; whether or not they're
fixed; and even their "status" in the ranks of dogs—via
pheromone-secreting glands located all over their bodies, as well as through their excretions. Urine and feces
are the real informational motherlodes, and this is why
dogs will ration their urine on walks—they're trying to
reach the widest possible audience. Even dogs who have
never met in the flesh but have daily walking routes that

overlap "know" each other. Similar, perhaps, to how we "know" the people in our DIY Home Renovations on a Budget Facebook group.

We'd probably be amazed to know all that dogs have gleaned about *us*, just from our smells. Our emotional states are surely transmitted pheromonally, which may be why dogs sometimes seem prescient of our moods. Dogs are also capable of picking up on sickness, chemical imbalances, pregnancy, and whether a terminally ill person is nearing death, though most have to be trained to interpret these olfactory inputs. Far from simply tracking, dogs' impressive noses have been tasked with missions ranging from military to medical: bomb detection, cancer detection, low blood sugar detection for diabetics, and impending-seizure detection for epileptics are just a few examples.

—————————————— Taste ——————————————

Dogs have limited taste receptors compared to humans (1,700 taste buds to our 9,000), though they're able to experience, with less intensity, the full range of human-detectable flavors, including sour, bitter, salty, sweet, and spicy. Dogs derive pleasure from sweets, but most exhibit a strong aversion to artificial sweeteners. They also have additional receptors for meats and fats, and, like many other animals, dogs can "taste" water.

Like humans, dogs' sense of taste is closely linked to smell, though in their case it's probably much more so. Dogs even have an olfactory organ on the roof of their mouth. Though its purpose isn't entirely understood, this *Jacobson's organ* may play a role not only in taste and smell but also in mating drive and emotional processing.

Hearing

Canine hearing is another standout sense for the species, at least compared to humans. Dogs can hear both lower and much, much higher frequencies—our hearing range encompasses 20–20,000 hertz, whereas a dog's range (depending on breed and age) is 15–65,000 hertz. This is why dog whistles, which emit a frequency of about 35,000 hertz, work, even though we can't perceive them, and why things that seem auditorily benign to us can agitate dogs—our shower singing voices, distant thunder, the vacuum cleaner, etc.

While humans have six muscles in each ear, dogs have eighteen. And their dexterous, animated ears aren't just for cuteness and intrigue. Though they *do* use them to others' benefit (to signal their emotional states and social intentions, both to humans and other dogs), they also perk them up, press them down, and swivel them around—often independent of each other—as a means of isolating and localizing sounds.

Some claim that their advanced hearing even accounts for dogs' uncanny ability to "predict" natural disasters. In the case of earthquakes, in particular, studies suggest that dogs may in fact be hearing seismic activity outside the human auditory spectrum—i.e., the grinding and sheering that occurs as the earth's plates gear up for a big shake—in the days or hours leading up to a quake.

----------- Touch -----------

Of the five senses, touch is the one our two species experience most similarly. Like humans, dogs have pressure-sensitive nerve endings at the base of each hair follicle and, like us, have other receptors for pain, chemical stimulation, movement, proprioception (i.e., the position of our bodies in space), and temperature.

Dogs have long, extra-sensitive hairs on their snouts and around their eyes. These *vibrissae*—we may know them as "whiskers"—can register subtle shifts in airflow and pressure. Also especially sensitive are dogs' spines,

tails, and feet. Even their toenails, though seemingly rugged, are full of tender nerves. Many dogs will let none but their nearest and dearest, if any, handle their feet.

Administering long, firm strokes that target the muscles (rather than only stimulating the follicular nerves as is typical of lighter "petting") is an effective way to calm most dogs. A phenomenon called the *caress effect* even posits that stroking a pregnant dog in this manner has a similar calming effect on her unborn puppies, potentially setting them up to be mellower, less reactive dogs upon their entry into the world.

We may not even realize the deep bonding work that's transpiring during our petting and cuddling sessions, because they can be fairly routine. But touch between our two species is special, as it's perhaps the only place where we can meet, more or less, as sensory equals. It's the one language we both innately know— no interpretation or imagination needed—and, as such, the connections we forge via touch, though often below the surface of our perception, are profound.

CHIHUAHUA

BASSET HOUND

BULL TERRIER

GREYHOUND

MASTIFF

THE CANINE IMAGINARY: WHAT MAKES A DOG A DOG?

I magine you've been tasked with explaining "a dog" to someone who's inexplicably never seen or heard of one. How would you describe it? How would you convey what is essential about *dogness* accurately, vividly, and succinctly?

Most of us can probably describe the basic physical characteristics of a dog: four legs with short-toed paws at the ends, a long-ish tail, fur, two prominent ears, two far-apart eyes, and a snout.

And if you've ever lived with dogs, you could likely map out their personalities in great detail—over time, we develop an innate sense of their needs, wants, and aversions; what motivates them; what they're communicating with certain behaviors. My dog Winnie loves chasing her Frisbee and has a perplexing aversion to windsocks. She needs near-constant physical affection and lots of exercise. She wants badly to please me, so she's motivated by praise. But also food. When she crawls into my lap and starts licking my face, it means it's 10:30 p.m. Biscuit o'clock.

And just like that, we've gotten to the bottom of what a dog "is."

. . . Or have we?

As we've established, when we take DNA out of the equation, dogness can be difficult to pin down. There's no standardized list of universal traits, nor is there any single characteristic we can point to and say, "dog, definitely."

The previous physical description *could* be a dog. But it could also be a wolf, a fox, or a coyote. Even a cat in soft focus. And if we were to expand the description to include more specific traits—a flattened snout, large bulging eyes, a curly-cue tail—we'd then run into the opposite problem. Not all dogs are pugs.

The dog personalities we know so intimately are of course anomalies, too. Even between my two dogs, the differences are stark. Ramona lives for sunbathing, novel smells, and scavenging vaguely edible things from the yard. She couldn't care less about a

Frisbee, or about pleasing me. While Winnie's a Velcro pup, Ramona is . . . more discerning. When I call her, she stands at a safe distance and stares at me as she does her calculations—what's in it for her if she comes? She'll approach only if she believes a treat (carrots are her favorite) or an excursion are impending. If I accidentally use the wrong tone of voice—too desperate or too cunning—she's off like a shot in the opposite direction.

Dogs certainly are an interesting case. Because of our influence, they're quite unlike all other canids. But then they're quite unlike us, too. We can't explain things to them—what existential threat we're facing, or that we'll be home from our work trip on Monday—nor can we ever know what it is to live in their technicolor world of smells.

And yet, because selective breeding has produced such an astounding variety of breeds, dogs are even quite unlike themselves. The most varied land mammal, they come in seemingly endless shapes and sizes, each with different aptitudes, drives, behaviors, temperaments, and preferences.

To complicate things further, dogs, like humans, are individuals. Not every person likes chicken, though it's been a staple of the human diet for thousands of years. And though it's the basis for most human social interaction, not everyone is comfortable making eye contact. Some people prefer firm beds while others prefer soft ones. It's the same with dogs. Even those born from the same litter and raised in the same home will have their differences.

THE SEVEN
BREED GROUPS

I t's out of necessity that we often resort to talking about "the dog" as if it were a kind of hive mind—a single conglomerate being portioned out into numerous furry bodies, all the same. Without generalizations, how could we talk—or write or read—about them? Here we'll get more specific as we look at smaller groupings of dogs—called breed groups—as well as a curated selection of individual breeds. Though this will still be reductive to some extent—each dog is a sovereign creature, after all—we can begin to narrow things down *a lot* when we look at dogs this way.

For the uninitiated, breed groups are larger categories used to organize individual breeds, and each group typically contains breeds of related function and form— what purposes they were originally bred for (i.e., hunting versus sitting on laps), their lineage, and/or their shared traits.

Breed groups are far from an exact science. They're determined by the canine kennel clubs of the world, and each organization has their own way of doing things. Here we'll be exploring those set by the American Kennel Club (AKC), which uses seven different breed groups: Hound, Herding, Working, Sporting, Nonsporting, Terrier, and Toy. Each of the 197 dog breeds currently recognized by the AKC has a place in one of these seven groups.

By contrast, 355 breeds are recognized by the Fédération Cynologique Internationale (FCI), which is the largest international canine organization, representing nearly 100 national kennel clubs globally. Their classification system is a bit more nuanced with ten breed groups: Sheepdogs and Cattledogs (except Swiss Cattledogs), Pinschers and Schnauzers, Terriers, Dachshunds, Spitz and Primitive Types, Scent Hounds and Related Breeds, Pointing Dogs, Retrievers/Flushing Dogs/Water Dogs, Companion and Toy Dogs, and Sighthounds.

Though originally conceived for the purpose of standardizing pedigree and streamlining dog shows, breed groups can be informative for casual dog lovers as well. Learning the roles that a dog's ancestors were bred to serve can be helpful for anticipating—and making sense

---

of—certain behaviors. Herding dogs often have a biological imperative to nip at people's heels, a behavior that seems odd if you don't know that they were bred to keep livestock in line this way. Understanding breed groups can also give us insight into keeping our dogs stimulated and optimizing their training.

❧ ❧ ❧ A NOTE ON "PURE" BREEDS ❧ ❧ ❧

An obvious limitation is that only purebred dogs are accounted for here. Of course, not all dogs are composed of just one breed—in fact, most of the world's dogs aren't. To keep any dog's breedline pure requires a tremendous amount of human intervention. Dogs don't ask to see each other's pedigree papers when left to their own devices.

Even so, breeds and breed groups essentially represent building blocks for all our domesticated dogs. It can be fun to mix and match typical breed and breed group characteristics with what we know about our nonpurebred pups and to use the information like a diagnostic tool. A dog that sees red in the presence of a robin or squirrel might be responding to the primal urges of their inner terrier. One that's liable to abscond as soon as they catch a whiff of something might have some hound in them. And a dog that compulsively bites the vacuum as you're cleaning the house could very well have the ghost of a herding dog ancestor whispering provokingly in their ear.

Keep in mind, too, that nearly all of today's "purebreds" were once mixed breeds themselves. A mix can be considered "purebred" after several generations of controlled breeding between dogs of the same ilk (though the road to becoming AKC or FCI recognized is more involved). *Controlled* breeding is key here, though. Mixes that are the product of accidental or natural breeding aren't usually purebred contenders—as a mix's makeup becomes more and more eclectic through generations of indiscriminate interbreeding, the dogs that result are true originals, all but impossible to replicate, let alone standardize.

HOUNDS

The hound group, along with the working group, houses some of the oldest known dog breeds. The basenji, for instance, is estimated to be at least 6,000 years old. Hounds, like terriers, are hunters. But while terriers are the ratcatchers of dogdom, most hounds are in the business of large game. True to their name, wolfhounds were bred specifically to take down wolves, and in the case of the Afghan hound, their quarry included leopards and gazelles.

Hounds are further divided into two subgroups: sighthounds and scenthounds. *Sighthounds* were bred for acute long-distance eyesight, whereas *scenthounds* were bred for their ability to track prey via their noses. This division accounts for significant physiological differences, as well.

In addition to their keen eyes, **sighthounds** are built for speed and endurance. They needed to be able to spot the movement of prey on the horizon and then run it down. As such, their bodies are typically lithe with aerodynamic lines, and their legs are long and powerful. They gallop rather than trot and can run long distances without tiring.

Scenthounds, on the other hand, are slow and steady. Their sense of smell is off the charts, even for a dog. They track an animal by the microscopic particles it leaves behind. A scenthound's body, therefore, is heavier and stouter, designed to maintain contact with the earth. They trail with their heads down and their long, heavy ears brushing the ground to rustle up any nascent scents that might be useful.

Hounds as a group are intelligent and independent, verging on stubborn. They are highly trainable, but successful training requires patience. Interesting sights or scents can easily overtake them. They need a lot of exercise and mental stimulation.

Some hounds employ a unique vocalization known as *baying*, which is a loud, undulating sound somewhere between a bark, a howl, and a yelp. Historically, this is how they would let hunters know they had cornered prey, though many still use the sound today to signal excitement, frustration, or even boredom.

The hound group includes breeds such as the beagle, the borzoi, the bloodhound, the basset hound, the greyhound, the saluki, and the whippet, among others. Here we'll take a closer look at two hound breeds: the dachshund and the Irish wolfhound.

DACHSHUND

AVERAGE HEIGHT: 8–9 inches (standard) / 5–6 inches (miniature)

AVERAGE WEIGHT: 16–32 pounds (standard) / 11 pounds or less (miniature)

LIFE EXPECTANCY: 12–16 years

Also known as wiener or sausage dogs for their long, muscular bodies and short legs, dachshunds are the smallest of the hound group. They've consistently ranked among the top dog breeds in the Western world for over seventy years, and have even garnered something of a cult following for their endearingly disproportionate bodies and their feisty, "big dog" personalities.

Dachshunds are bold, independent, and lively. With their short legs, they're not great distance runners or skilled jumpers, but they're active and playful and, like most hounds, have a strong prey drive and like to chase things, whether that be toys, skateboards, or cats.

This small scenthound is the most varied of the purebreds. They come in two sizes, according to the AKC—standard and miniature—though the FCI recognizes an even smaller third size: the *kaninchen*, or rabbit, which tops off at just 10 pounds. And, unofficially, any dachshund that falls between 12 and 16 pounds is known in the "doxie" community as a *tweenie*. Further distinction is made based on their coats: there are smooth, longhaired, and wirehaired dachshunds.

Even though dachshunds are "small" dogs, it's unwise for owners to forgo proper training and socialization. They also need plenty of physical and mental stimulation. Under-socialized or under-stimulated dachshunds can quickly turn snappy and destructive. Dachshund rescues abound with poor pups whose owners mistook the hound for an "easy," hands-off pet due to their manageable body size.

Dachshunds are prone to unhealthy weight gain, perhaps owing to the fact that they're often misrepresented as toy dogs due to their size and subjected to low-activity lapdog lifestyles. In these instances—compounding the problem—dachshunds may resort to food for the stimulation they crave.

—————————— **Historical Highlights** ——————————

Natives of Germany, dachshunds date back to at least the fifteenth century and may be the product of selective breeding between miniature pointers and pinschers, though others claim they're descendants of the bloodhound. A fascinating hybrid-esque breed, dachshunds were designed to have the tracking abilities of a scenthound, but in miniature form, with proportions closer to a terrier. And like terriers, they're something of a big dog in a little dog's body; what they lack in size they make up for with their big, sometimes confrontational personalities. In the FCI, dachshunds are considered anomalous enough to warrant their very own breed group.

The name *dachshund* reveals the breed's original purpose—in German, *dach* translates to "badger," and *hund* to "dog." Dachshunds' uniquely long bodies and short legs enabled them to pursue badgers into their holes. Their large rib cages protected their organs in the compact underground spaces, and their big lungs allowed them to retain oxygen. (As a side note, these big lungs also lend them a much louder bark than their size would suggest!) The miniature dachshund was bred for smaller prey, like rabbits.

Badger hunting was dangerous work, and dachshunds needed to be intrepid and feisty. You can see this devil-may-care streak in them today when they pick fights with dogs at the park twice their size.

During both World Wars, the German dachshund briefly fell out of favor within allied countries. During

World War I, some dachshund devotees even redubbed them "liberty hounds" to distance the dog from its controversial German heritage.

———————————— Hall of Fame ————————————

Kaiser Wilhelm II, the last German emperor, owned two dachshunds—Wadl and Hexl—who earned international notoriety when they savaged a treasured golden pheasant belonging to Archduke of Austria-Hungary Franz Ferdinand.

IRISH WOLFHOUND

AVERAGE HEIGHT: 32 inches (male) / 30 inches (female)

AVERAGE WEIGHT: 120 pounds (male) / 105 pounds (female)

LIFE EXPECTANCY: 6–8 years

Considered "gentle giants," Irish wolfhounds are a serene and affectionate breed. They are vigilant and can be protective of those they love but are not naturally aggressive toward people. The breed *does* have a strong prey drive baked into their DNA—they're sighthounds after all!—so cats and other small animals might disagree on the point of their gentleness.

Irish wolfhounds are the tallest breed recognized by the AKC, standing up to three feet at the shoulder, and up to seven feet when on their hind legs. Though they're not the heaviest breed on record, they can get up there—it's not unheard of for an adult male to reach 180 pounds, which is heavier than most wolves. They have wiry, medium-length coats and scruffy, whiskered faces. They are both strong and graceful, and at a gallop they are capable of impressive speed.

Due to many health issues common in the breed, the average life span of the Irish wolfhound is sadly quite short. Only 9 percent make it to the age of ten. As with other large breeds, Irish wolfhounds are susceptible to both gastric torsion—aka bloat—and hip dysplasia.

They also tend to be stoic, even when in pain, so don't always show signs of illness while treatment is still an option.

For their tremendous lovability combined with the briefness of their mortal frolic, they've even been nick-named "the heartbreak dog" by those who have had the honor of sharing their lives with these majestic creatures.

———————— **Historical Highlights** ————————

Of Celtic origin and dating back to as early as 400 BCE, the Irish wolfhound was a prized breed in the ancient world. Widely renowned for their grand size and valor, they were used most commonly for hunting large game like wolves and stag, though many accounts have also placed them on the battlefield, employed for the purpose of dragging enemies from their horses. These sight-hounds were often presented diplomatically as gifts to nobility and royalty abroad; we first see mention of them in a letter from 391 CE, written by Roman statesman Quintus Aurelius Symmachus to his brother, thanking him for the gift of seven "Irish hounds." Across the centuries that followed, they were the frequent subject of poems, songs, and stories, where they were exalted to mythical proportions for spectacular acts of bravery and loyalty.

Though the Irish wolfhound is one of the oldest breeds on record, the dog as we know it today is, in fact, a reproduction. The original Irish wolfhound went extinct near the end of the eighteenth century.

The modern iteration was designed in Gloucester, England, during the second half of the nineteenth century. Captain George Augustus Graham—a Sottish soldier and dog breeder—purportedly commissioned a life-size illustration of the lost breed, which he used as his model. After two decades of trial and error, Graham eventually created his fantastic amalgamation through interbreeding the Scottish deerhound (believed to be a relative of the first Irish wolfhound), the Great Dane, the Tibetan mastiff, and the Russian wolfhound, or borzoi.

Graham's "invention" was controversial among his Victorian peers, though in time the reimagined Irish wolfhound came to be considered once again a highly desirable purebred companion.

Just as the original Irish wolfhound found himself at home among the royals and highborn of yore, the "new" Irish wolfhound seems to have followed suit: U.S. Presidents Herbert Hoover and John F. Kennedy both owned Irish wolfhounds while they were in office. The dogs' names were Patrick and Wolfie, respectively.

HERDING DOGS

It wasn't until 1983 that the AKC gave herding dogs their own category. Previously, they were included in the working group, which makes sense—herders are intelligent, hardworking dogs, who are happiest when they have a job to do.

What differentiates those in the herding group is their inborn ability to command other animals, even those much larger than they are. Though plenty have adjusted to the pampered pet life, many of these dogs are still employed today herding cows, sheep, horses, and reindeer.

Herders are alert, observant dogs, with a keen eye for subtle changes in their environment, though not all of these breeds work the same way. Australian cattle dogs, or heelers, will nip at the heels of cattle as a means of directing them while Beaucerons use their gaze and body language. And some of these dogs are used primarily for protecting vulnerable livestock from predators or shepherding flocks through inclement terrain.

On average, these energetic dogs require more dedicated attention than other breeds. Not only do they need lots of physical activity, but they also need their minds engaged. When bored or pent-up, they can become neurotic and destructive. Because of their sensitivity to their surroundings, many function best with reliable routines and consistency. That said, they're also dynamic, adaptable dogs who delight in learning new things.

Breeds in this group include the German shepherd, the Australian shepherd, the Canaan dog, the Spanish water dog, the Finnish lapphund, the mudi, the puli, and the Old English sheepdog, among others. Here we'll explore two herding breeds in detail: the border collie and the Pembroke Welsh corgi.

BORDER COLLIE

AVERAGE HEIGHT: 19–22 inches (male) / 18–21 inches (female)

AVERAGE WEIGHT: 30–55 pounds

LIFE EXPECTANCY: 12–15 years

Border collies are medium-size sheepherding dogs with boundless energy and an insatiable desire to please. Whether they're managing sheep in the English hills or fetching the newspaper, these dogs live for their to-do lists and positive reinforcement. When a job isn't provided for them, borders may take it upon themselves to create one—digging holes in the yard, perhaps, or systematically chewing off all the kitchen baseboards.

Border collies can seem almost psychically keyed in to their owners, as they were bred to detect subtle command cues from the farmers and herders who reared them. Often considered the smartest of all breeds, their intelligence lends them an intensity that can be too much for some. They were engineered to command flocks in part by staring at them. Without a flock to watch, they use their gaze to communicate with those around them. To be the subject of a border collie's steely, unbroken stare is an enthralling and inexplicably discomfiting experience—as if it dredges up ancestral memories of glassy eyes peering out at you from the darkness just beyond the encampment.

This isn't the only thing wolf-like about them, either. The way they herd is similar to how wolves hunt. Using a technique we call *modified predatory*, they stalk, crouch, and nip, stopping short of lunging in for a kill. Border collies' shoulder blades are even uniquely structured, with a little extra space between them, allowing the dogs to move with precision while in a crouched position. This maneuver is sometimes referred to as the *border collie crouch*, though a few other herding breeds do it as well.

With their strong, limber bodies and penchant for problem-solving, borders excel at agility training and obstacle courses, and they regularly take home the gold in sheepdog trials. Individual borders can vary quite a bit in both size and appearance. While most commonly black with white markings, they can also be bicolored, tricolored, or merle, and their thick double-coat can be medium-length and feathered or short and coarse.

Borders are susceptible to a non-life-threatening condition called *border collie collapse*, also known as "the wobbles," which is not fully understood—after a combination of physical exertion and elevated mental excitement (playing fetch with a favorite ball, say), some borders will become disoriented, begin dragging their back legs, and eventually need to lie down. Physical exercise isn't enough to trigger it, though; they also need to be excited. Several other herding and working breeds also experience "the wobbles."

———————— **Historical Highlights** ————————

Working collies—the predecessor to border collies—have a long history of herding and protecting sheep in the rocky hills of Scotland and northern England, where the nimble, hardy sheepdogs were ideally suited for the cold, craggy, expansive terrain. It's said the word *collie* is an old rural Gaelic word meaning "useful." Precisely when these early collies appeared is up for debate, though there's evidence they were proving their usefulness as early as the Middle Ages, if not before.

The border collie first came into the public eye in the 1890s, when a black-and-white dog from Cambo, Northumberland, began dominating sheepdog trials in the region. His name was Auld Hemp (Old Hemp), and observers were stunned not only by his flawless trial record but also by his uniquely subdued herding style. While sheepdogs of the day typically relied on their voice to command, Old Hemp used his speed and body language. His owner, Adam Telfer, claimed the prize-winning dog hadn't required any training—his abilities were innate. Everyone wanted their own little Old Hemp, and he became a prolific stud dog. Old Hemp—who lived from 1893 to 1901—is believed to have sired more than 200 dogs. All purebred border collies of today can trace their bloodline back to Old Hemp.

It's very possible that Old Hemp wasn't the first of his genetic makeup. Some say, for instance, that Queen Victoria's collie Sharp, born in 1854, was in fact a border. But for the combination of his intelligence, natural abilities, and gentle temperament, Old Hemp was certainly one of a kind, and it's these qualities that became the blueprint for what we prize about the breed today. Border collies have been popular dogs ever since Old Hemp's debut, though it wasn't until 1995—a hundred years later—that the breed was officially recognized by the AKC.

A border collie named Chaser from Spartanburg, South Carolina, garnered international fame for her expansive vocabulary—she was recorded as knowing over 1,000 words. Chaser, who passed away in 2019 at the age of fifteen, was considered by many to be the smartest dog in the world.

PEMBROKE WELSH CORGI

AVERAGE HEIGHT: 10–12 inches

AVERAGE WEIGHT: 30 pounds or less (male) / 28 pounds or less (female)

LIFE EXPECTANCY: 12–13 years

Not unlike the dachshund, the Pembroke Welsh corgi is a long-bodied, short-legged dog with a distinctive silhouette. Also similar to the dachshund, they're at the smaller end of their breed group and tend to have big-dog energy in little-dog form. Though the *other* corgi—the Cardigan Welsh corgi—does have common dachshund ancestry, the Pembroke likely bears no relation. The two corgis were interbred for many years, but it's since been determined that the Pembroke and Cardigan are entirely separate breeds, with different regional and ancestral histories, despite their physical similarities. Pembrokes are the more popular of the two.

Pembrokes are cow dogs, though their role has often been that of "reverse" herder, meaning they keep neighboring livestock from encroaching on their territories. As such, they can be territorial, manifesting as a high "stranger danger" drive. While they're not naturally aggressive, they can be big barkers. With a Pembroke, you're likely to always know when the mail's been delivered.

These sporty, cheerful little dogs have big heads for their body size and distinctly fox-like facial features.

Historically their tails have been docked to keep them from getting stepped on by cattle, though some are now bred to be naturally tailless.

Due to their herding dog intelligence, proper training and socialization are essential, and though they're lower maintenance than some of the other herders, they still require daily exercise and play. Pembrokes will often engage in a behavior known as frapping, or, colloquially, "doing zoomies," where they'll tire themselves out running in circles or zigzagging from room to room.

Historical Highlights

There are two possible origins of the Pembroke Welsh corgi. By some accounts, they're not *true* dogs at all, but visitors from another realm—the realm of fairies and elves. This explains their unearthly cuteness, their foxiness, and the saddle-shaped markings that many of them have on their backs—fairies apparently ride corgis and have them pull their little carts.

The other theory relates to King Henry I of England's love of fine tapestries. In the early twelfth century, Flemish weavers were at the top of their class, and

King Henry I, eager for easier access to their talents, invited a group of them to take up residence in Wales. The weavers brought with them their small Flemish cattle herding dogs, which in time became the Pembroke Welsh corgis of today. Pembrokes are believed to be a delightful hodgepodge of the keeshond, the schipperke, the Pomeranian, the Samoyed, the chow chow, the Norwegian elkhound, the Finnish spitz, and perhaps others.

Hall of Fame

Pembroke Welsh corgis were famously the favorite breed of Queen Elizabeth II. She was gifted her first Corgi, Dookie, by her father in 1933 and had a revolving cast of Pembrokes in her life from that point on—most of them the product of her own royal corgi breeding program. She was said to have owned more than thirty Pembroke purebreds, plus a few "dorgis," or dachshund and corgi mixes, during her lifetime.

WORKING DOGS

This group includes some of the most ancient breeds, and, as suggested by the name, working dogs are the blue-collar laborers of dogdom. Their kind have pulled our sleds and carts, guarded our homes, and protected our families and livestock against wolves, panthers, and human intruders for millennia. They've also been employed as watchdogs, service dogs, police dogs, and rescue dogs. Many working dogs still serve these purposes today. The only type of doggy-designated labor they *don't* have a paw in is herding, since herders now occupy their own category.

Working dogs are, almost without exception, *big* dogs. They're also intelligent and—like herders—eager to learn, which makes them highly trainable. That said, the protective and predatory instincts so deliberately bred into them can require skill to redirect. And, considering their powerful size, it's crucial that training not be taken lightly. For these reasons, many aren't ideal for casual or first-time pet owners.

The working group consists of the Bernese mountain dog, the boxer, the Doberman pinscher, the Great Dane, the dogue de Bordeaux, the komondor, the Newfoundland, the rottweiler, and the Samoyed, among others. Here we'll get better acquainted with two working breeds: the Akita and the Mastiff.

AKITA

AVERAGE HEIGHT: 26–28 inches (male) / 24–26 inches (female)

AVERAGE WEIGHT: 100–130 pounds (male) / 70–100 pounds (female)

LIFE EXPECTANCY: 10–14 years

Traits and Temperament

The heavy-boned, heavy-coated Akita is a loyal, digni-fied dog. Their big heads and small, dark features lend the breed a serious, alert expression. They have fluffy, curled tails that flop over onto their backs. Originating in the snowy mountains of northern Japan, Akitas love snow and are most comfortable in milder climates.

Akitas were bred to hunt big game, including the Jap-anese Yezo bear, and guard nobility, and these fearsome instincts are still present in them. A loving, doting family pet, the protective Akita's not typically as keen on strang-ers. While this hypervigilance can be a deterrent for some potential owners, for others it's an upside—as long as an Akita's on site, one can trust that their house, yard, and loved ones will be amply guarded. And many Akita lovers claim the inconveniences are well worth what they receive in return: an affectionate, gentle compan-ion whose devotion is absolute. Because of their guard dog history, Akitas tend to rank high on lists of most aggressive breeds, but happy, healthy, well-trained, and well-socialized ones aren't typically a threat to people. Many are even used as service and therapy dogs.

Akitas are not the "dog people" of dogs. On average, they seem to prefer human company. Because they can be aggressive with other dogs—especially those of the same sex—they tend to do best in a one-dog household and aren't always dog-park contenders. They'll gladly take their exercise at the end of a leash, however—a solid daily walk is usually enough for these pups.

Most Akitas aren't barkers under normal circumstances, but when relaxed at home, they can "mutter" or "grumble" as they go about their business. They also exhibit a behavior called mouthing—an Akita hallmark—where they delight in carrying things around in their teeth and will even gently redirect a member of their family with their mouths if they feel they're getting skimped on attention. Akitas are uniquely fastidious and groom themselves by licking, like cats.

According to the AKC designation, the breed includes two different types: the Akita Inu (or Japanese Akita) and the American Akita. The American Akita is a slightly larger, more modern version of the ancient Japanese Akita. Japanese Akitas are fox-like, whereas the American Akita tends more toward "giant teddy bear."

The FCI and other kennel clubs now consider them two separate breeds.

─────────── **Historical Highlights** ───────────

Though the saluki currently holds the Guinness World Record for the "oldest dog breed," some researchers believe that several breeds—including the early Akita—are actually older. Either way, the Akita is a dog of most ancient stock, though their precise origin remains something of a mystery.

Hailing from the wintery mountain regions of Japan's Akita prefecture, today's iteration of the Akita can be traced back to *at least* the seventeenth century, where the breed was a tightly controlled status symbol among Japanese nobility. General citizens weren't permitted to own them until the nineteenth century.

In the 1930s, Akita Inus were officially made a national treasure by the Japanese government. Despite this prestige, their numbers dwindled bleakly during World War II. With strict rationing orders in place, many Japanese families could no longer feed their dogs—especially ones as large as the Akita—and the breed teetered near extinction. Luckily, enough made it to the end of the war for repopulation efforts to be successful.

Still considered a national treasure, Akitas even have a spiritual significance in their native country—they symbolize health, happiness, and a long life. When someone has a baby or falls ill, a small Akita Inu statue is often gifted to them for luck.

—————————— **Hall of Fame** ——————————

Hachiko—an Akita born in 1923—is possibly the most famous dog in all of Japan. He would accompany his owner, Professor Ueno, to Tokyo's Shibuya train station each morning to see him off to work and would go back each evening to wait for Ueno's return train. Tragically, Ueno died suddenly while at work one day, and for ten years, Hachiko—or Hachi, as Ueno called him—returned to the platform day after day, stoically waiting for his owner to reappear. In 1934, not long before Hachi's own death, a bronze statue was erected in his likeness at the Shibuya station. Though the original statue was melted down for use in war efforts during World War II, a second one replaced it and still stands today.

American author and disability rights advocate Helen Keller is reputedly responsible for introducing the Akita to the United States. When Keller visited Japan in 1937, she was so moved by Hachi's story that someone gifted her an Akita puppy. When the puppy, named Kamikaze, died of distemper shortly after arriving in the States, Keller was sent a replacement—Kenzan, Kamikaze's younger brother—who was her companion for many years.

MASTIFF

AVERAGE HEIGHT: 30 inches or more (male) / 27.5 inches or more (female)

AVERAGE WEIGHT: 160–230 pounds (male) / 120–170 pounds (female)

LIFE EXPECTANCY: 6–10 years

Though there are many mastiff-*type* dogs, the Mastiff—
also known as the English mastiff or Old English mastiff—is distinguished by the capital "M." Mastiffs are
known first and foremost for their mass—their name
even comes from the Anglo-Saxon word *masty*, meaning "powerful." The powerful, towering Mastiff can be as
tall as three feet at the shoulder and can easily tip the
scales at more than 230 pounds.

But as any Mastiff lover will tell you, their looks
are—to some extent—deceiving. While they *do* have a
protective side that requires proper training and socialization to mitigate, once Mastiffs reach adulthood, their
default setting is that of tenderhearted lazybones.

What's more, well-bred, well-trained Mastiffs seem to
have an intuitive sense of what other creatures might be
a legitimate threat to them or those they care for, and
they are exceedingly gentle with anyone—animals or
people—smaller than them. They love children and are
known to be patient with little dogs haranguing them.
They are also famously friends of cats, birds, and other
diminutive, non-canine house pets.

Mastiffs are drool machines and can be gassy. They also snore, often loudly. In lieu of barking, which they do infrequently, they sigh and groan expressively. They sadly don't live very long, on average, though it's not unheard of for a Mastiff to surprise everyone by living well into their teens. Like other large breeds, they're especially susceptible to both bloat and dysplasia.

Mastiffs are big babies, literally and figuratively. They don't reach full maturity until three years of age; for dogs who don't frequently live past ten, their puppyhood represents a sizable chunk of their lives. Intelligent and people-pleasing, they're also sensitive. They spook easily and tend to sulk when reprimanded or when they feel left out. And they're stubborn—there's no forcing a full-grown Mastiff to do something they don't want to do.

Historical Highlights

Though today's Mastiff is a product of nineteenth-century Great Britain, the aforementioned mastiff-type dogs have been around much, much longer. In the earliest days of human civilization, some believe there were three essential "types" of dogs: thick-coated northern sled dogs, light-boned sighthounds—similar to today's greyhound—and giant, muscular dogs—similar to modern mastiff-types. These early mastiffs have been dubbed Molossian hounds after the Molossian tribe of ancient Greece, where they may have originated. The mythical Cerberus is believed to be one of these "Molossers."

Most of our mastiffs today—the English mastiff, but also the Neapolitan mastiff, the cane corso, and the dogue de Bordeaux, among others—are offshoots of this original mastiff-esque dog. They both evolved and were crossbred over millennia to produce pups more suited to the environs and circumstances in which they found themselves in.

The British Isles possibly encountered their first mastiffs in the sixth century BCE, via Phoenician traders, and there's evidence that when Rome attempted invasion some 500 years later, the Roman legions were so impressed with the giant, fearless dogs the British had fighting alongside them that they brought a pack of them back to Rome.

Many of our Mastiffs today can be traced to the beginning of the fifteenth century, to a female legendary for protecting her owner, the knight Sir Piers Legh, as he lay wounded on the field during the Battle of Agincourt. The name of the Mastiff herself is lost to time, but her prodigious litter was dubbed the Lyme Hall Mastiffs, after Legh's home, where the puppies were born.

Over their long history, Mastiffs have been employed as guard dogs, war dogs, attack dogs, rescue dogs, hunters, beasts of burden, and shepherds. Infamously, they were weaponized by Christopher Columbus and the conquistadors and used to terrorize the native peoples of the Americas. They've also been put to extensive use in fighting and baiting—both in the arenas of ancient Rome, where they faced bears, bulls, lions, gladiators, and each other, and, less ceremoniously, in pits and gambling dens.

After dog fighting was banned in Great Britain in 1835, ferocity and aggression were no longer prized in the breed, and the Mastiff began to take its current form as a kindly, mild-mannered companion. Like the Akita, the rationing of World War II took a dramatic toll on the giant breed, and Mastiffs nearly died out in Great Britain. After the war, Americans shipped over Mastiff breeding stock to kick off repopulation efforts, which thankfully were successful.

————————————— **Hall of Fame** —————————————

The largest dog on record was a Mastiff named Zorba, who lived from 1981 to 1992. Full-grown he was 37 inches high at the shoulder, and 8 feet 3 inches long from his nose to the tip of his tail. He weighed 343 pounds.

One of the passengers on the Mayflower was a Mastiff, belonging to a pilgrim named John Goodman. Goodman, along with half of his travel companions, didn't make it through his first Plymouth winter. His dog did, however, and we know from written firsthand accounts that the Mastiff was adopted and cared for by other colonists.

SPORTING DOGS

Sporting dogs—also known as gun or bird dogs—have been bred to work closely with hunters to flush out, find, and/or retrieve felled game. They're naturally alert and innately companionable. Smart and athletic, many perform equally well on land and in water. Like the Labrador retriever and the Portuguese water dog, some have webbed feet and water-resistant coats, which keep their fur from weighing them down while swimming. Sporting dogs are still used on hunts, though their intelligence and how in tune they are with humans make them ideal family dogs, too. Several breeds have also found their niche as service dogs.

This group is broken down into four "types," based on the breed's job description. As the name indicates, **retrievers** were developed to retrieve game for hunters, both on land and in water. **Pointers** scent out prey and "point" to what they find by freezing in place and angling their muzzle toward it. **Setters** are also scenters and will freeze in a crouched position—called a *set*—to indicate that they've found something. **Spaniels** are primarily used to flush out prey from their hiding places. Then there is a fifth miscellaneous group, for breeds that don't fit exactly into any one "type" but are skilled hunters nonetheless.

This group includes the barbet, the bracco Italiano, the Brittany, the cocker spaniel, the English setter, the Irish setter, the Nova Scotia duck tolling retriever, the pointer, the vizsla, and the Weimaraner, among others. We'll now shine a spotlight on two sporting breeds: the golden retriever and the Nederlandse kooikerhondje.

GOLDEN RETRIEVER

AVERAGE HEIGHT: 23–24 inches (male) / 21.5–22.5 inches (female)

AVERAGE WEIGHT: 65–75 pounds (male) / 55–65 pounds (female)

LIFE EXPECTANCY: 10–12 years

Golden retrievers are the quintessential "good boys." This much-loved, medium-size dog continually ranks in the top five for most popular breeds, and for good reason: they're intelligent, highly trainable, kid-friendly, and they have gentle, easygoing personalities. It doesn't hurt that they're lookers: Goldens, as they're often called, are athletic, well-proportioned pups with flowing golden-yellow coats and feathery tails that stand joyfully upright. Their faces are open and friendly, with dark, expressive eyes.

Because these dogs were bred to retrieve waterfowl, their desire to play fetch can be insatiable, and they love to swim. Also, for this reason, they're "mouthy" and will often carry things around in their mouths throughout the day—sticks, toys, a random sock—and might hold their own leashes as they're walked. What's more, they're known for their especially "soft" mouths and possess an odd talent: a golden can apparently cup a raw egg in its mouth without breaking it.

For their intelligence and even temperament, golden retrievers are frequently trained as service dogs. They also make great therapy dogs and excel at search and rescue. Like all sporting breeds, goldens require plenty of exercise and love to be outdoors.

They're also *big* eaters, so feeding should be controlled. Anything remotely edible is best kept out of their reach, especially when they're left home alone—the breed is infamous for swiping loaves of bread and baked goods off the kitchen counter or stealing the butter from the dinner table.

Historical Highlights

For how much we love our goldens, it feels like they've been with us since the beginning. And yet we've only been graced with their existence for a little over 150 years.

For a long time, goldens were rumored to be descendants of Russian circus dogs. However, the breed is Scottish in origin, developed between 1835 and 1890 by a man named Dudley Marjoribanks (aka Baron Tweedmouth) whose careful breeding records were shared with the public by his nephew in 1952.

From these records we learned that golden retrievers are the product of a yellow retriever named Nous and a tweed water spaniel (a now-extinct breed) named

Belle, who gave birth to a serendipitous litter of amiable, golden mixed-breed puppies in 1864—Crocus, Primrose, and Cowslip. This then-new breed continued to be fine-tuned over the years—perhaps Irish setter and bloodhound were also eventually added—and entered its first dog show in 1908.

--- **Hall of Fame** ---

In 1974, President Gerald Ford was given a golden retriever, whom he named Liberty. After Liberty's arrival, the popularity of the breed skyrocketed in the United States, and it has remained at the top of the doggy charts ever since.

Bretagne was a golden retriever who, along with around 300 other specially trained dogs, participated in the Ground Zero search and rescue mission in the days following 9/11. Bretagne—pronounced "Brittany" earned recognition for being the last living dog of the 9/11 crew, before she died in 2016, just shy of her seventeenth birthday.

NEDERLANDSE KOOIKERHONDJE

AVERAGE HEIGHT: 16 inches (male) / 15 inches (female)

AVERAGE WEIGHT: 20–30 pounds

LIFE EXPECTANCY: 12–15 years

Considered a rare breed outside of Europe, the Nederlandse kooikerhondje (pronounced "NEY-der-lands COY-ker-hond-che") is a relative newcomer to the AKC scene. The kooiker, also known as the Dutch spaniel or Dutch decoy spaniel, is a small but sturdy spaniel-type dog with a long, silky, red-and-white coat. Their waterproof fur repels dirt and grime easily, so despite the kooiker's luxurious look, they're actually very low-maintenance dogs in terms of grooming. The kooiker's ears and tail are perhaps its most distinguishing characteristics: the tips of many kooikers' ears look as if they were dipped in black ink—a feature referred to as *earrings*—and the mostly white tail is plush and excessively feathered.

The cheerful, affectionate kooiker is also very intelligent—some say it rivals even the border collie in smarts—and easily trained. They're emotionally in tune with their owners but can be aloof around strangers, at least at first. They can also be reactive with unfamiliar dogs, and even the most enthusiastic of kooiker lovers agree they're not typically dog-park pups. Luckily, there are other ways to engage and exercise these athletic little dogs—they tend to excel at agility training and doggy sports like flyball. Kooikers have a strong prey drive and will often go after smaller animals, though they usually do okay with cats they've known since puppyhood.

———————— Historical Highlights ————————

The Dutch Nederlandse kooikerhondje is far from a new breed but still relatively unknown in the United States. They were added to the AKC registry in 2018 and, as of 2022, there were less than 500 registered kooikers in North America (to put this into perspective, there are nearly 100,000 Labrador retrievers registered in the United States alone). It's unclear exactly when these dogs first appeared. Though they feature in seventeenth century paintings by Dutch masters like Johannes Vermeer and Jan Steen, it's likely that they predate their high art debuts by a couple centuries.

During the Middle Ages, when duck was a staple of many Europeans' diets, duck peddlers used kooikers to lead ducks into elaborate pond-system traps called *eendenkooi*. The dogs' fancy white tails served as lures, and the ducks would follow them to their unwitting demise. During their off-hours, the dogs were also used as exterminators.

As technology advanced and *eendenkooien* dwindled, so did the breed. By the early twentieth century, kooikers were few. While many European breeds took a hit during World War II, the kooiker conversely made its comeback. The Baronesse von Hardenbroek van Ammerstol, in silent resistance to the Nazi occupation of the Netherlands, began a discreet breeding program for the Dutch breed. Between 1942 and 1976, she produced over fifty kooiker litters, single-handedly bringing the breed back from the brink.

—————————— Hall of Fame ——————————

Prince Willem van Oranje, founder of the Dutch monarchy, purportedly had a kooiker that saved his life during an assassination attempt in 1572—the little dog alerted him of the attack in time for Prince Willem to escape. Some claim the dog's name was Kunze, and others say his name was Pompey. There's also some debate about whether the dog might have been a pug.

NONSPORTING DOGS

The nonsporting group is something of a catchall and includes diverse breeds from various backgrounds. Many of these breeds have served a specific purpose historically, but they're now primarily considered to be companion animals or show dogs. Some find themselves in this group simply because they don't meet the weight requirements for the toy group, so nonsporting dogs range in size from fairly small, like the Tibetan spaniel and the bichon frise, to quite large, like the chow chow and the dalmatian. On average, these dogs need less exercise than those in the preceding groups, though there are certainly exceptions.

Other breeds in this group include the Boston terrier, the bulldog, the Chinese shar-pei, the keeshond, the Lhasa apso, the Norwegian lundehund, and the schipperke. Let's take a closer look at two nonsporting breeds: the standard poodle and the Xoloitzcuintli.

STANDARD POODLE

AVERAGE HEIGHT: 18–24 inches

AVERAGE WEIGHT: 60–70 pounds (male) / 40–50 pounds (female)

LIFE EXPECTANCY: 10–18 years

Known for their ornate hairdos and associations with French aristocracy, these frequent dog show champions are one of dogdom's more divisive breeds. Poodles are often seen as dainty, decorative dogs, analogous with the vanity, frivolity, and ostentatious wealth of the leisure class. After the 2020 Westminster Kennel Club Dog Show, where a black standard poodle named Siba beat out the crowd favorite—a golden retriever named Daniel—for the title of Best in Show, social media was abuzz for weeks with impassioned takes. Many saw Siba's victory over a ruddy, well-liked sporting dog as evidence that high society was, once again, being unjustly favored over the working class. Of course, there were at least as many who celebrated her triumph—for all the flack the breed catches, there's no dearth of die-hard poodle fans (in fact, poodles currently rank as the fifth most popular dog in the United States).

Though poodle devotees (like devotees of all breeds) are perhaps drawn to them in part for their aesthetic, there's more to the breed than their flamboyant silhouette. Poodles are *highly* intelligent dogs. They respond beautifully to training and are eager to please and perform. Throughout history, the breed has served many purposes, their roles often overlapping with those of working and sporting dogs. They're athletic and have a knack for doggy sports of all kinds. They also love to swim.

The poodle's gentle, easygoing demeanor makes them an excellent family dog, and their unique hypoallergenic coat means they're a great option for those who may not be able to live with a dog otherwise. Poodles have hair rather than fur, so they don't shed. While a plus for many, this also contributes to their high-maintenance reputation—the breed needs regular grooming to keep their coats from matting or growing too long.

Poodles come in three sizes—standard (over 15 inches tall), miniature (10–15 inches), and toy (less than 10 inches)—with each size considered a separate breed rather than a variation of the same breed (as we saw with dachshunds). Standard and miniature poodles are both considered nonsporting dogs while toys are registered, fittingly, in the toy group.

Poodles are true renaissance dogs. Not only has their intelligence and athleticism made them a jack-of-all-trades breed, but poodles were also literally born out of the Renaissance period, even finding themselves immortalized in the era's art: a Rembrandt painting from 1631, titled *Self-Portrait in Oriental Attire with Poodle*, features a large scruffy member of the breed in the foreground, as one example.

Though they are commonly associated with France (even holding the title of "Chien National de France"), poodles actually originated in Germany in the 1400s, where they were used for centuries as retrievers of waterfowl. The word *poodle* comes from the German *pudelin*, an onomatopoeic word meaning to splash about in water.

Even the fussy, impractical-seeming poodle hairstyle—the so-called continental clip, with the coiffed lion's mane, the ball-of-fluff tail tip, and the conspicuous leg warmers—once served a practical function. Less hair allowed the dogs to move more easily in water, but in their native Germany, they also needed protection from the cold. Hunters shaved them down where they could and left bands of fur to insulate their joints and vital organs.

Because of its unique coat, the poodle was historically a frequent contributor in breed design—the Irish water spaniel and Portuguese water dog are examples of poodle offshoots. For the same reason, they've also become the stars of the contemporary "designer mix" world. Though the purebred poodle may be maligned at times, we sure do love our goldendoodles, our Labradoodles, and our Yorkie-poos.

Aside from retrieving felled ducks, poodles also excelled as circus performers, truffle hunters, service dogs, and therapy dogs. A team of standard poodles was even used to compete in Alaska's Iditarod Trail Sled Dog Race in 1988. Though the dogs may have been up to the task otherwise, they weren't cut out for the icy, subzero temperatures. Some of the dogs nearly froze and had to be dropped off at checkpoints. In response, Iditarod officials revised the entrance qualifications, and now only cold-hardy northern breeds are allowed to compete.

Charles le Chien, aka Charley, was a French-born standard poodle who belonged to *Grapes of Wrath* author John Steinbeck. In 1960, Charley accompanied Steinbeck on a 10,000-mile road trip across the United States, which Steinbeck documented in his book *Travels with Charley: In Search of America*.

XOLOITZCUINTLI

AVERAGE HEIGHT: 10–14 inches (toy) / 14–18 inches (miniature) / 18–23 inches (standard)

AVERAGE WEIGHT: 10–15 pounds (toy) / 15–30 pounds (miniature) / 30–55 pounds (standard)

LIFE EXPECTANCY: 13–18 years

The Xoloitzcuintli (pronounced "shoh-loh-eats-QUEENT-lee") is famous for something it doesn't have: fur. Though, in reality, there are coated varieties of the breed—about one in five puppies will be born with a short, sleek coat—and even the hairless ones typically have a bit of coarse hair, most often on their feet or tails, or a sparse tuft on top of their heads. Both the coated and hairless dogs come in an assortment of colors, such as black, red, bronze, gray, or gray-black, and they can be solid or spotted. Also called the Mexican hairless, or simply the Xolo, the breed additionally stands out for its large, bat-like ears and, oddly, its dentition. The genetic mutation that causes baldness also affects their teeth, and hairless Xolos are usually short a few of the requisite forty-two. Some members of the breed can also develop especially long, protruding incisors, called tusks.

Xolos are intelligent, loving, and loyal companions, and they make good watchdogs. Because their vigilance means they are naturally wary of strangers, others might not understand what love bugs these unique-looking dogs really are. They're considered a calm, dignified breed and aren't excessive barkers. Another breed with a strong prey drive, they should be watched around cats and other small animals. And it might be a good idea to keep an eye on them in general—they're also excellent escape artists.

The Xolo comes in three sizes: standard, miniature, and toy. Even the smallest Xolos are strong, hardy dogs. Past puppyhood, Xolos' exercise needs are very manageable—for most, a daily walk will do. But due to their (usually) hairless bodies, they're more sensitive to weather than most. They require sunscreen, and sweaters are in order during colder months. Many smaller Xolos' owners will even litter box train their pups to minimize their exposure to winter elements. Native to the jungles of Central America, Xolos live for summer—on warm days, you'll often find them lazing serenely in the sun, almost catlike.

—————————— Historical Highlights ——————————

A national treasure of Mexico, the Xoloitzcuintli is one of the oldest dog breeds in the world—dating back at least 3,000 years, and maybe more. Artifacts depicting

Xolo-like dogs have been found in ancient Mayan and Toltec tombs. Some believe that when humans first arrived in the Americas via the Bering Strait, they brought the predecessors of today's Xoloitzcuintlis with them (though the gene for hairlessness that has become the breed's trademark would likely have appeared later).

They are one of a number of so-called *primitive* breeds, meaning they weren't selectively bred by humans to look or behave or perform a certain way, and were allowed to evolve naturally. For this reason, Xolos are extremely rugged and healthy dogs, evidenced by their long life span.

Xolotl was the Aztec god of fire, lightning, and death, and *itzcuintli* translates to "dog" in the Aztec Nahuatl language. This breed was sacred to the Aztec, who believed that the dogs served as Underworld guides. When Xolos' owners died, the dogs would be sacrificed and buried alongside them, to steward them safely into the next life. There's evidence that the Aztec also ate Xolo meat, though not as an everyday dish; sacred, it would have been reserved for ceremonial feasts.

Historically, Xolos have been attributed mystical healing powers. Even today, some believe that the breed is able to prevent and cure such ailments as arthritis, asthma, toothaches, and insomnia. Mystical potential aside, there may be some truth to their ability to at least soothe, if not heal: their hairless bodies radiate warmth, like little hot water bottles.

This breed was one of the first dogs recognized by the AKC—in 1887, under the name "Mexican hairless"— though in the 1950s it was removed from the registry due to its waning numbers. In 2011 the dog was added once again, this time by its proper god-given moniker: *Xoloitzcuintli*.

——————————— Hall of Fame ———————————

Mexican artists Diego Rivera and Frida Kahlo owned several Xolos during their tumultuous twenty-five-year marriage, and the dogs made appearances here and there in their artwork. Kahlo's favorite dog, Señor Xolotl, is featured in her 1949 painting *The Love Embrace of the Universe, the Earth (Mexico), Myself, Diego, and Señor Xolotl*.

TERRIERS

Terriers are the rat catchers of the canine world. The name *terrier* comes from the Latin *terra*, meaning "earth," and many of these spunky pups were bred to take care of pests at the source: by digging or dragging them out of their cozy, hard-to-reach burrows. It was dangerous work—especially for the smaller breeds—and tenacity, ferocity, and outsized courage were requirements to get the job done. Terriers aren't as active in the extermination business these days, but these qualities are still present in them and referred to as "terrier fire."

Stubborn and barky, they can go into pursuit mode on a hair trigger. They're intelligent dogs who respond well to training, but their attack-dog instinct means that any training is liable to go out the window at the sight of squirrels, birds, or other small, skittering animals. This group encompasses three different "types" of terriers, each bred for a different function.

Short-legged terriers are the true "earthdogs" of the

group and perhaps what we picture most readily when we hear the term *terrier*. These dogs—the Scottish and the cairn are two examples—are built low to the ground, with flexible spines for burrowing and powerful jaws and needle-sharp teeth for detaining and thrashing vermin. Designed to be able to wedge themselves into spaces too tight for their human counterparts, they had to work without direction. Consequently, for better or worse, many of these little dogs have a fierce independent streak.

Long-legged terriers, like the Airedale and the Parson Russell, are the product of long-ago interbreeding of short-legged terriers with leggier hounds or sporting dogs. With their bigger bodies and stronger legs, these terriers were made to access their quarry from aboveground, by digging. These versatile dogs held other jobs, too, besides pest control: retrieving, herding, and guarding were all possible side hustles for long-legged terriers, and some were used on hunts to course rabbits and bolt foxes and badgers.

Bull-type terriers were developed in Great Britain in the eighteenth and nineteenth centuries through mixing terriers with larger, more muscular dogs. The objective was to design the ultimate canine fighter—the strength and bite force of a larger dog combined with the agility and fearlessness of a terrier—to savage competition in the brutal, high-stakes world of animal fighting. Though most modern bull-type terriers are sweet and stable pups, centuries of bad press mean many people are still wary of these "fighting" breeds.

Now we'll focus in on two very different terrier breeds: the bull terrier and the Dandie Dinmont terrier.

BULL TERRIER

AVERAGE HEIGHT: 21–22 inches

AVERAGE WEIGHT: 50–70 pounds

LIFE EXPECTANCY: 12–13 years

The distinctive-looking bull terrier—with its stocky build, football-shaped head, and small, black, triangular eyes—rose to fame in the late twentieth and early twenty-first centuries as the marketing mascot for two big U.S. name brands. As Bud Light's Spuds MacKenzie and Target's Bullseye emerged as household names during this time, so did the bull terrier breed. (As a side note, Bullseye has even been rendered in wax—you can find her doppelganger on display at Madame Tussauds in New York City.)

Bullies are energetic, companionable dogs. Fans of this breed love them for their playful personalities, their loyalty, and their indiscriminate friendliness. Bullies are obsessed with people and do best in homes where they're permitted to be at the center of the action. Their rambunctiousness and curiosity lend them a serious "life of the party" energy—a quality that certainly wasn't lost on Bud Light's marketing executives.

This signature feistiness can have its downsides, and bull terriers who aren't properly trained and socialized can become bossy, possessive, jealous, and aggressive toward other dogs. An active breed, they need plenty of exercise. A bored or lonely bullie can be quite destructive. They can also succumb to obsessive behaviors such as pacing, spinning, or excessive tail-chasing, especially when unhappy or under-stimulated. And, owing to their terrier heritage, they're stubborn, which means training a bullie isn't for the faint of heart.

Bullies have an endearingly jaunty gait and an easy-to-groom short coat that can be all white or "colored." They also come in miniature. At 10 to 14 inches in height and 23 to 33 pounds, miniature bull terriers are about half the size of larger bullies, and, though they're still classified in the terrier group, they're considered a separate breed by the AKC. (Bullseye is actually a miniature bull terrier, for the record.)

─────── Historical Highlights ───────

Animal fighting didn't immediately cease to exist when it was banned in Great Britain in the 1830s. Like most outlawed pastimes, it went underground. For many years, dogs still fought each other gruesomely to the death in taverns and cellars countrywide while onlookers gambled on the outcome.

Many of these pit-fighting dogs were a potent combination of the old English bulldog and various English terriers of the day. These so-called *bull-and-terriers* were larger and stronger than terriers, but quicker and more intrepid than bulldogs. Though the term itself is no longer in use, the bull-and-terrier became the blueprint for all modern bull-type terriers, including the bullie.

Eventually, authorities managed to crack down on illegal dogfighting, and, out of necessity, many bloodsport breeders pivoted their breeding programs. As there was no longer a reliable market for aggressive dogs, breeders had to get creative with their inventory. Thus, "masculine" but aesthetic and companionable breeds began to take form.

John Hinks is credited with masterminding the early bull terrier. His intent was to create a strong-looking dog that was also dignified and elegant—a "gentleman's dog." In the 1850s, using his white Old English bulldog, named Madman, and the now-extinct English white terrier, Hinks devised the bullie base. Over time, he mixed in dalmatian, English pointer, and whippet to improve grace and agility.

Hinks' all-white bull terriers—"white cavaliers," as he called them—made quite the impression on the Victorian dog world. After Hinks' death, others continued to tweak the breed, with the most notable addition being that of the Staffordshire bull terrier, which accounts for the variety of coat colors we see in the breed today.

—————————— Hall of Fame ——————————

A deaf bull terrier named Patsy Ann was once named the official greeter of Juneau, Alaska. Patsy Ann was born in 1929, and for her sensory limitations she possessed a curious ability: She always knew exactly when ships were arriving and where on the wharf they would dock. With no permanent home of her own, she spent her days welcoming the ships' crews and paying visits to her favorite locals. At night she slept in the Longshoreman's Hall. For her unique talent and outgoing personality, she was much adored. In 1992, fifty years after her death, a bronze Patsy Ann statue was erected on the very wharf where she once sat each day awaiting new friends.

Though most of us are familiar to some degree with cool-guy beer-hound Spuds MacKenzie, fewer know the dog behind the dog. Spuds was in fact a female bull terrier named Honey Tree Evil Eye, or "Evie." Born in 1983, Evie spent the first few years of her life as a Chicago show dog before making her commercial debut for Bud Light in 1987. She died of renal failure in 1993, at the age of nine.

DANDIE DINMONT TERRIER

AVERAGE HEIGHT: 8–11 inches

AVERAGE WEIGHT: 18–24 pounds

LIFE EXPECTANCY: 12–15 years

Like most terriers, the Dandie Dinmont is a study in opposites: the sweet, scruffy, bright-eyed face that belies an inner exterminator of legendary proportions; the silky white topknot and feathered ears that sail glamorously on the wind as the Dandie runs after a squirrel, intent on thrashing it; the demure, compact body that houses a startlingly loud, baritone bark.

In silhouette, the exceptionally rare Dandie Dinmont could be mistaken as a relative of the dachshund or the corgi for its long-bodied, short-legged shape. True to its earthdog roots, it's a sturdy, rugged dog with a plucky attitude. These sharp little pups are calmer than other terriers in their size class, and they're loyal, with warm, responsive personalities. That said, they're also independent adventurers who resist coddling, and they can be willful. Training a terrier is often a sizable task, and the Dandie, despite its mellower presentation, is no exception. With its alert mind and big bark, a Dandie makes an excellent watchdog.

Dandies' coats come in one of two shades: pepper (black to light silvery gray) or mustard (reddish to golden brown). They need regular brushing to keep their fur from matting and trims to keep their faces clear, but they're minimal shedders.

<hr>

Historical Highlights

Dandie Dinmont terriers are one of the rarest AKC breeds and are considered an endangered native breed in the United Kingdom, though repopulation efforts are underway. They're also one of the older terrier breeds, dating back to at least the 1700s, though their lineage is speculative at best. They hail from the border region between England and Scotland, and Scotland claims the dogs as their own. Like most terriers, Dandies were born of humble beginnings, earning their keep as vermin-catching farm dogs. In particular, the breed has a knack for dispatching otters.

Early on, Dandies were referred to by various names: Catcleugh, Hindlee, or pepper and mustard terriers, after their coloring. Sir Walter Scott, notable Scottish author, had a soft spot for these funny little terriers and cast them as characters in his novel *Guy Mannering*. The protagonist of the book, a man named Dandie Dinmont, owns several. After the book's publication in

1815, the dogs became known commonly as Dandie Dinmont's terriers, though the possessive "s" was eventually dropped.

Some believe the character of Dandie Dinmont was based on a Scottish farmer named James Davidson, who, at one time, owned six Dandies, known as "the immortal six." It's possible that all Dandies today come from two of Davidson's dogs, Tarr and Pepper, though this claim has been contested.

Hall of Fame

King Louis Philippe of France was a noted fancier of the Dandie Dinmont terrier. He supposedly kept a small pack of them and traveled with at least two at all times as part of his royal entourage.

TOYS

All breeds in the toy group have in common their diminutive size—they typically don't exceed 15 pounds, and many are much smaller—and, unlike dogs in other groups that were initially bred with a rough-and-tumble job in mind, the primary function of toys has, for the most part, always been human companionship. As such, these pups were designed to be cheerfully disposed and lightweight enough to be picked up and carried around. While a portable "purse" dog might seem like a contemporary invention, several of these breeds—such as the shih tzu and the Maltese—are ancient.

Because of the limited space these dogs take up, they're commonly the group of choice for apartment dwellers and frequent flyers who prefer to bring their pups with them when they travel. On average, these breeds need less exercise than larger dogs, so can be a good option for people with less active lifestyles. Daily playtime plus a walk or two will do the trick for most—after all, with their shorter legs, they're taking more steps than we are. But just because they're easier to physically manage doesn't mean that training and socialization should be skimped on. Toy breeds may not be at risk of seriously injuring someone if an interaction goes awry (compared to an Akita or Mastiff, for example), but structure and stimulation are critical for *any* dog's health and happiness. Small dogs can still become timid, fearful, and aggressive if these needs aren't addressed. Training can also be a positive bonding experience between dog and owner—something small dogs crave, perhaps more than most. Bred to be good company above all else, toy breeds have evolved to be quite dependent on their humans, both physically and emotionally.

Some breeds in the toy group include the Brussels griffon, the Cavalier King Charles spaniel, the Chihuahua, the miniature pinscher, the Pomeranian, and the Yorkshire terrier. Here we'll do a deep dive into two toy breeds: the Italian greyhound and the pug.

ITALIAN GREYHOUND

AVERAGE HEIGHT: 13–15 inches

AVERAGE WEIGHT: 7–14 pounds

LIFE EXPECTANCY: 14–15 years

The Italian greyhound, or Iggy, is the miniature version of one of the oldest known sighthounds. This graceful, upbeat dog is famous for its shy, sweet demeanor and love of creature comforts. But despite its penchant for warm laps and cozy blankets, the Italian greyhound is no couch potato. Iggies have the instincts and bodily proportions of full-size greyhounds, and that highly developed prey drive, combined with their long-legged lightning quickness (Iggies can easily reach 25 miles per hour when they get going), means that they pose a serious flight risk. Categorized as a toy breed due to their size, it's important to remember that these dogs are still bona fide sighthounds at heart.

Though their small-boned bodies might look unnervingly fragile, they're physically hardier than they appear. They're also playful and active, and not afraid to get their paws dirty. That said, their short coat and minimal body fat provide little in the way of insulation, making them especially vulnerable to the cold, which may account for their hallmark snuggle-seeking tendencies. Another benefit of the short coat is that they hardly shed and grooming is a breeze. However, whatever time Iggy owners save on grooming should go into caring for their teeth, as they are prone to dental problems and need their teeth brushed regularly.

Italian greyhounds are social and affable—they bond closely with their families and tend to get along well with other dogs. They're intelligent and exceptionally sensitive, which can tip over into a nervous disposition if they don't feel safe in their environment. Their sighthound alertness makes them reliable watchdogs, but they're likely to scamper off if the threat draws too close. These little dogs are lovers, not fighters, through and through.

———————— Historical Highlights ————————

The Italian greyhound is an old and prolific breed, with origins that resist being pinned down. Archaeologists have traced their lineage back at least 2,000 years to the areas Greece and Turkey occupy today, where, in addition to companionship, they would have been employed as small-game hunters and perhaps also served as pest controllers before the advent of the terrier class.

But there's evidence that the breed—or at least an ancestor that closely resembles it—goes further back.

Some claims place Italian greyhounds in Mesopotamia and ancient Egypt, as early as 3000 BCE—a theory based on remains of entombed dogs recovered from Egyptian pyramids, of which some are strikingly similar in size and skeletal structure to today's Iggy.

They may have also, like mastiffs, made a cameo in Greek mythology. In one myth, the goddess Artemis turns the hunter Actaeon into a stag when he accidentally comes upon her bathing. And, as if that weren't punishment enough, Actaeon's hounds—who many believe to be miniature greyhounds—mistake their cursed master for ordinary quarry and tear him limb from limb. This scene plays out famously on a fifth century BCE relic: a painted vase, currently housed at the Museum of Fine Arts in Boston, that depicts Actaeon being pulled to the ground by his four small, leggy dogs, while Artemis stands over him with her bow drawn.

More recently, Iggies made a name for themselves—quite literally—in Renaissance Italy. During this era, owning miniature versions of larger dogs was an Italian status symbol and Iggies were adored by the Italian upper classes. This led the dogs to be featured in the works of several well-known Italian Renaissance painters, and it's this Italian fine art spotlight that earned them their current moniker. From here, their popularity spread throughout the upper echelons of the wider European continent—Catherine the Great and Queen Victoria are rumored to have been Iggy owners during their reigns.

But what they were so revered for—their tininess—also almost became their undoing. As Iggies were bred to be smaller and smaller, the resulting dogs became progressively less healthy, until eventually the breed was but a sickly shadow of its former self. Toward the end of the nineteenth century, breeders were able to restore the Iggy back to its original robustness, though the glory was somewhat short-lived.

Like so many other breeds, the Italian greyhound was a near casualty of the wars of the twentieth century, and after World War II the Iggy's outlook was bleak in Europe. Thankfully, owing to another round of purposeful breeding endeavors (and with some help from American breeding stock), the European Iggy population was eventually rebuilt.

Upon a visit to Johannesburg in the second half of the nineteenth century, South African Matabele king Lobengula Khumalo was so charmed by someone's pet Italian greyhound that he offered to buy it from him. When the man initially refused, a bidding war ensued. Lobengula did take the sought-after pup home with him in the end, but it cost him 200 cattle—one of the highest prices ever paid for a dog.

PUG

AVERAGE HEIGHT: 10–13 inches

AVERAGE WEIGHT: 14–18 pounds

LIFE EXPECTANCY: 13–15 years

Traits and Temperament

Pugs are known the world over for their wrinkly, smushed faces, their raspy snorts, and their lovey-dovey, low-maintenance personalities. These petite, muscular dogs have big heads with small velvety ears, short corkscrew tails, and prominent, expressive eyes.

Their short coats are easy to care for, and pug advocates (of which there are *many*) call them the perfect house dog. Well-adjusted pugs seem to get along with everyone—kids, the elderly, other dogs, and cats. But as with every dog, big or small, pugs rely on training and socialization. Even with their perennially sweet temperaments, fearful pugs can be neurotic, skittish, and even aggressive with strangers (though a pug's "aggression" is usually vocal—they're all bark, no bite). Very smart, they can be willful and mischievous at times, especially when they feel they're being deprived of the attention that is their toy dog birthright.

Pugs' unique physiology means that they're prone to some unique health issues. The fore-shortened snout—a canine trait known as *brachycephaly*—can cause breathing problems, and their protruding eyes are susceptible to injury. In particular, pugs are at risk for a condition called *proptosis*, where the eye partially pops out of the socket, which can happen if too much pressure is applied to the neck (from straining against their collar during a walk, for instance). Their wrinkles can also collect grime and harbor bacteria, so need to be cleaned regularly to avoid skin infections. Pugs' large heads, while a contributing factor to their supreme cuteness, also make labor difficult on pug moms, thus many pugs are brought into the world via cesarean section.

Extreme heat should be avoided with pugs; due to their brachycephalic snouts, they're unable to regulate body temperature effectively through panting, so they overheat easily, which can be dangerous. Lastly, pugs have big appetites, and their stocky bodies can easily become overweight, so feeding shouldn't be a free-for-all. A trim pug isn't preferable simply for aesthetic reasons—obesity significantly increases the risks associated with any of the aforementioned health issues.

Pugs are another breed of deep antiquity, and, as such, we're again at the mercy of best guesses for piecing together their distant past. Though it's commonly accepted that the breed originated in China, the *when* and *how* get us. There's solid evidence that they've been around since *at least* the end of the Zhou Dynasty (ca. 400 BCE), but the breed may very well predate that by several centuries. Some believe that the now-extinct Chinese happa dog, who existed as far back as 1115 BCE and is predecessor to the Pekingese, may also be responsible for the pug. (And to see a picture of the grumpy-faced happa, with its flattened snout and bulging eyes, it's hard to not think "case closed!") Yet others assert that the pug is a miniaturized mastiff.

While we'll probably never know the whole story behind the first pugs, we do know they were highly prized in ancient China, and—along with the Pekingese and the shih tzu—were coveted companions of emperors and the very wealthy. In fact, pugs—known as *Lo-sze* in China—were so cherished by their keepers that many of them had their own servants, as well as guards to protect them against the very real threat of pug-napping. It's even rumored that during his rule in the second century CE, Emperor Ling bestowed his female pugs with the same rank as his wives. In addition to Chinese castles, there's evidence that pugs were also in residence at Tibetan monasteries during their early history, where they were similarly revered and perhaps also used as watchdogs.

In the sixteenth century, Dutch spice traders began returning from China with curious bonus cargo: small, wrinkled, irresistibly adorable dogs. It wasn't long before these Dutch mastiffs, as they were briefly called, became a must-have amongst the ruling classes of Europe. The pug's prominent role in post–Middle Ages European society is well documented in the art of the era, most notably in paintings. Francisco de Goya, François Boucher, and Antoine Pesne are just a few examples of painters whose works feature pugs.

From these renderings, we can even roughly trace the way the pug's appearance has changed over time. Though some depictions do closely resemble today's pugs, in others they're larger and longer-legged, with slightly longer snouts and curl-less tails. It's not clear whether the modern pug's peculiar morphology is a result of scattershot mixed breeding over the years or plainly an evolution of the breed itself (controlled or otherwise). As one of the first very small dogs abundant in Europe, we know that the pug *was* frequently inter-bred, but typically for the purpose of shrinking other breeds. Many of today's toy breeds have distant pug in their genome.

Other than their role as a miniaturizing ingredient (and the possible light sentinel duty in ancient monas-teries), pugs haven't ever served much of a "functional" purpose. Though the breed's popularity came under scrutiny for this very reason during its early days in the West—it was seen by some as a good-for-nothing sap on valuable resources (a parasite, in essence)—the trend caught on, and the question of whether a dog's company was reason enough to keep it was eventually outmoded.

It might be that the pug was the first breed to show us, on a grand scale, that a creature's worth isn't con-tingent on their material contributions to society. While many of us have come to accept this in our dogs—they don't need to *do* anything, we love them simply because they *are*—it's a notion that's often harder for us to accept about our own species. But does it have to be this way? Next time you feel down on yourself about your unfolded laundry, your unfinished degree, or a Sunday lost to scrolling, perhaps you'll find yourself meditating on the pug: the little dog who's never hustled, but who deserves to be here—and to be loved—as much as anyone.

―――――――――――――――― Hall of Fame ――――――――――――――――

When Joséphine de Beauharnais met her second husband, Napoleon Bonaparte, in 1795, she had already lived quite a life: her first husband, with whom she had two children, was executed in 1794 during the Reign of Terror, and she herself had spent several bleak months imprisoned at Les Carmes, awaiting a date with a guillotine that mercifully never came. During all this, Joséphine—known then as Rose—had an ill-mannered pug named Fortune who was very dear to her. It's said that while Rose was imprisoned, her children corresponded with her by tucking secret letters into Fortune's collar. The dog was smart enough to navigate the streets of Paris solo and petite enough to wriggle in and out of his mistress's cell.

As for his life as a Bonaparte, Fortune never warmed to his new father figure, and Napoleon purportedly bore a scar on his leg that he attributed to the small dog. Napoleon would joke that of all the enemies he'd faced, Fortune was the most formidable.

POSTSCRIPT:
NO SMALL GIFT

Loving dogs makes us think about time differently. History. Mortality. Personhood. What it means to be intelligent or "good." It's humbling, disorienting, and even sometimes frustrating, loving these beings we can't explain things to, whose minds we can't ever fully grasp. (I'd wager that it can be frustrating for them, too.)

Ramona, my older dog, had her tenth birthday a few days before I finished writing this book. I adopted her when she was nine weeks old, which means that I've been looking at her face nearly every day for almost ten years. Over a quarter of my life. Her face that was once solid black, which now wears a little white mask. I'm more familiar with it than I am my own.

To say I identify with her is an understatement; she's an integral part of my identity. Of course, she's also her own creature, barreling through the world on her own terms, guided by her nose, her whims, and her never-ending desire for treats. It's an extraordinary thing, accompanying a dog through all the phases of their earthly journey. *No small gift*, to use Mary Oliver's phrase. I knew Ramona as a baby, when I was a stand-in for a mother. Then for a while we were something like sisters. In the last year or so, she's started to feel more like an elder. I suspect she has a lot to teach me yet.